Extreme Sports

MOTOCROSS

Wendy Hinote Lanier

DiscoverRoo
An Imprint of Pop!
popbooksonline.com

abdobooks.com

Published by Pop!, a division of ABDO, PO Box 398166, Minneapolis, Minnesota 55439.

Printed in the United States of America, North Mankato, Minnesota.

052020
092020

THIS BOOK CONTAINS RECYCLED MATERIALS

Cover Photo: Shutterstock Images
Interior Photos: Shutterstock Images, 1, 8–9, 12, 18–19, 22, 23, 31; iStockphoto, 5, 6, 7, 17, 20, 21, 27, 28, 29, 30; Topical Press Agency/Hulton Archive/Getty Images, 11; History collection 2016/Alamy, 13; PA Images/Alamy, 14–15; Thurman James/Cal Sports Media/Zuma Wire/AP Images, 25

Editor: Brienna Rossiter
Series Designer: Jake Slavik

Library of Congress Control Number: 2019954956

Publisher's Cataloging-in-Publication Data

Names: Lanier, Wendy Hinote, author.

Title: Motocross / by Wendy Hinote Lanier

Description: Minneapolis, Minnesota : POP!, 2021 | Series: Extreme sports | Includes online resources and index.

Identifiers: ISBN 9781532167829 (lib. bdg.) | ISBN 9781532168925 (ebook)

Subjects: LCSH: Motocross--Juvenile literature. | Cross-country motorcycle racing--Juvenile literature. | Enduro motorcycle racing--Juvenile literature. | Extreme sports--Juvenile literature. | Sports--Juvenile literature.

Classification: DDC 796.046--dc23

WELCOME TO DiscoverRoo!

Pop open this book and you'll find QR codes loaded with information, so you can learn even more!

Scan this code* and others like it while you read, or visit the website below to make this book pop!

popbooksonline.com/motocross

*Scanning QR codes requires a web-enabled smart device with a QR code reader app and a camera.

TABLE OF
CONTENTS

CHAPTER 1

RACE DAY

The buzz of motorcycles fills the air. It sounds like a swarm of angry bees. A motocross event has just begun. The racers speed down the track on dirt bikes. They race toward the first sharp curve.

WATCH A VIDEO HERE!

Some motocross racers go more than 60 miles per hour (100 km/h).

The spray of dirt from a bike's tires is called a rooster tail.

The riders lean into the tight turn.

Their bike tires grip the rough ground.

Dirt sprays up into the air behind them.

The riders bounce over a series of small hills known as whoops. Then they reach a big hill. It sends them flying into the air.

Racers squeeze their bikes with their knees while riding through whoops.

More hills, jumps, and turns follow. The riders skid around the track's raised corners, called berms. Then they zoom toward the finish line. But the race isn't over yet. This is just the first lap. The riders

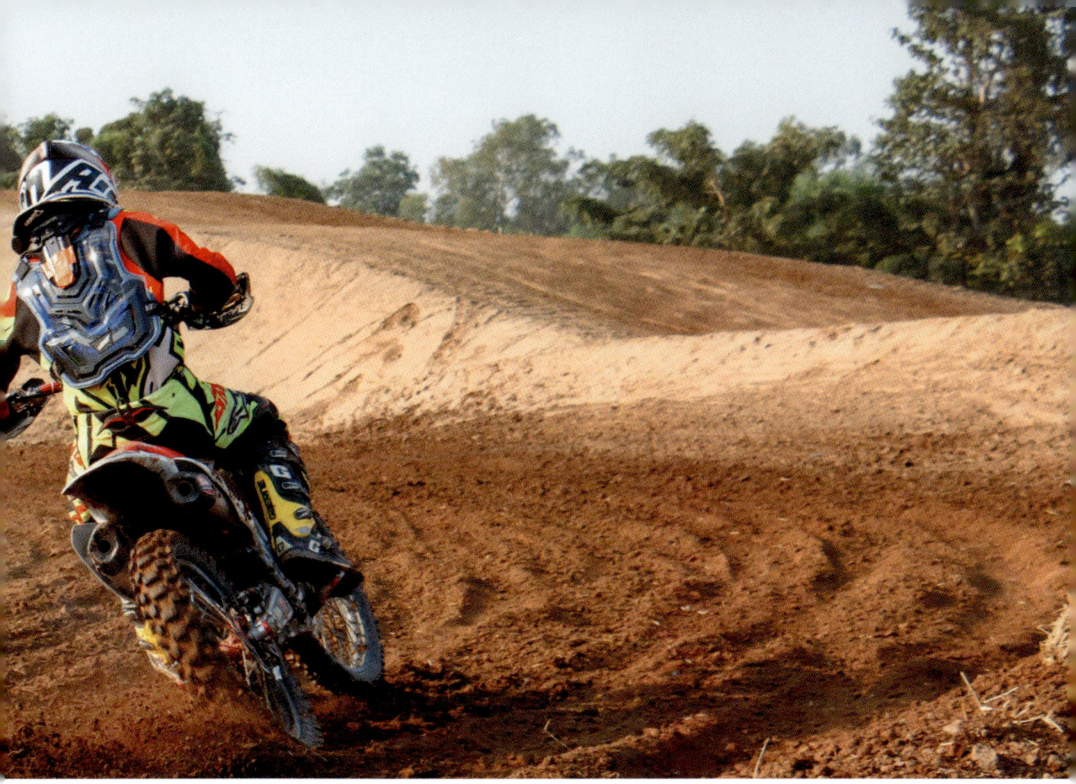

A banner marks the finish line. Racers ride under it to start the next lap.

will go through the whole course again several times.

DID YOU KNOW?

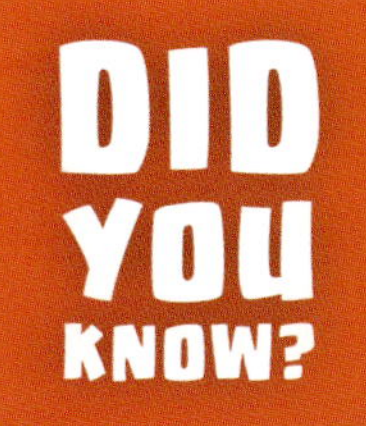

Most motocross tracks are between 0.5 and 2 miles (0.8 and 3.2 km) long.

CHAPTER 2

MOTOCROSS HISTORY

Motorized bikes were invented in the mid-1800s. In the early 1900s, they became known as motorcycles. Soon, **cross-country** motorcycle races were common in Europe. People raced over rough ground.

LEARN MORE HERE!

Riders race up a steep road during the Isle of Man Senior Tourist Trophy Race in 1912.

The 1920 Harley-Davidson Board Track Racer was built for speed.

After World War I (1914–1918), motorcycles became lighter and faster. People began holding new types of races called scrambles. These races used shorter, **closed-loop** courses. People marked the courses in forests or other natural areas.

By the 1950s, this style of racing was called motocross. This name combines the French word for motorcycle, *moto*, and the English word *cross-country*.

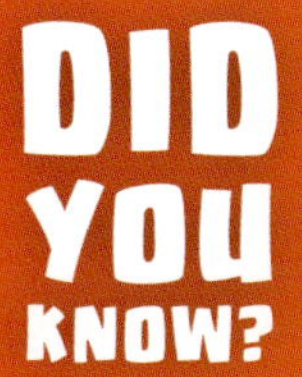

The first official scramble took place in England in 1924.

Spectators watch a scramble in the United Kingdom.

Swedish racer Torsten Hallman helped bring motocross to the United States in the 1960s.

In the 1960s, a businessman **imported** European dirt bikes to the United States. He also brought European racers to compete in motocross events. The sport became popular in North America. Many races were held in stadiums so that lots of people could watch.

CHAPTER 3

MOTOCROSS TODAY

Modern motocross races use dirt tracks. People add **obstacles** to make the tracks similar to **cross-country** races. Each track is a loop. Racers do several laps around it.

COMPLETE AN ACTIVITY HERE!

Obstacles often send racers flying into the air.

Some people race just for fun. Others race in competitions. Rules for motocross racing are set by the International

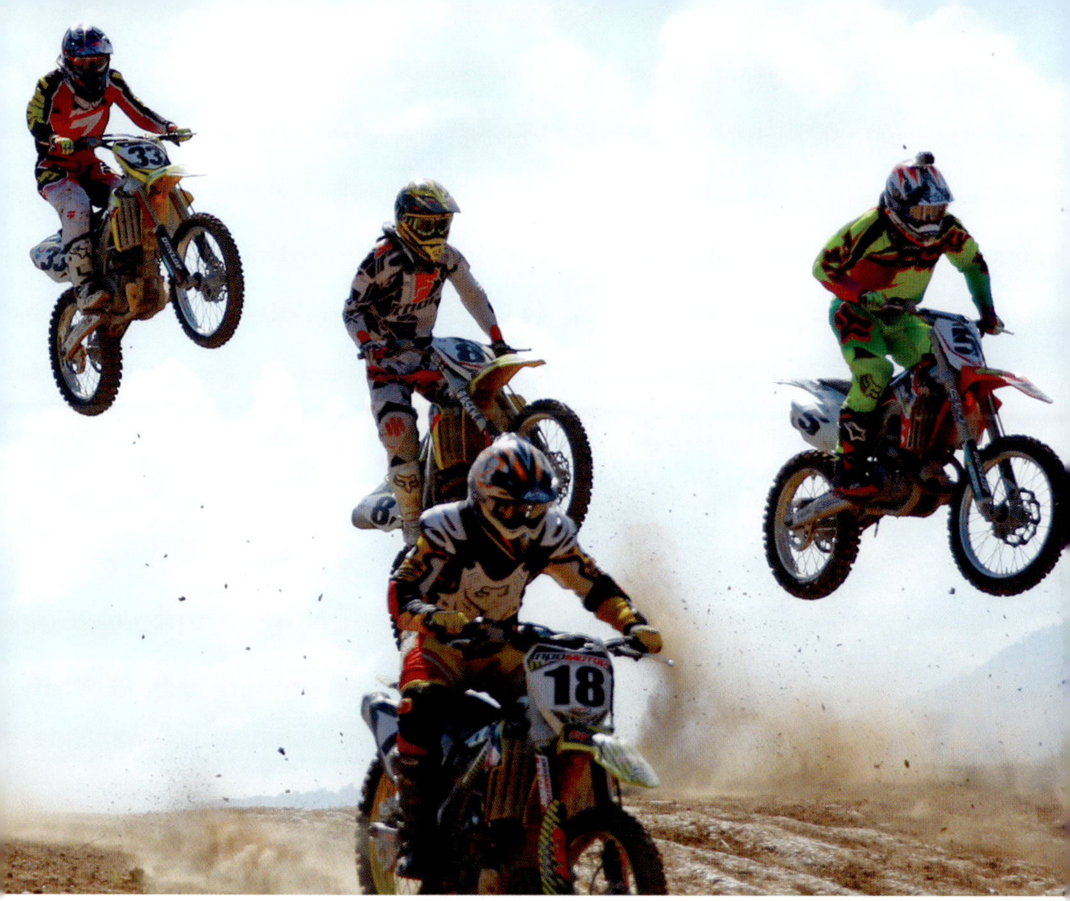

Racers compete in a championship race in Russia in 2014.

Motorcycling Federation. There are more than 100 racing groups around the world.

DID YOU KNOW?

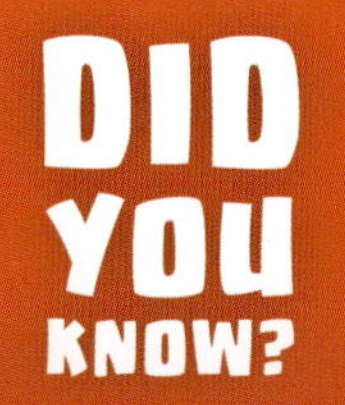

Some motocross competitions are for kids. Racers can be as young as four to six years old.

Most dirt bikes for adults are 32 inches (81 cm) wide. Bikes for kids are smaller.

Most professional motocross events have two classes. They are 250MX and

450MX. "MX" is short for *motocross*. The numbers tell the size of the racers' engines.

CLASSES AND ENGINE SIZES

For adults, motocross classes are set by engine size and rider experience. Engines are measured in cubic centimeters (cc). In the 250 class, engines are no more than 250cc. The 450 class uses bigger engines. They are 250cc to 450cc. Youth motocross classes are set by age and motorcycle size. The smallest bikes have 50cc engines.

Racers may crowd close together as they speed around the track.

Riders in each class race separately. Each race is made up of two **heats** called **motos**. Riders get points for their place in each moto. The rider with the most points after both motos wins the race.

In the United States, racing season is made up of 12 events. Riders earn points for their finish in each event. The person with the most points at the end of the season is the champion.

Some motocross events take place inside stadiums.

SUPERSTAR

ELI TOMAC

- Eli Tomac was born in 1992. His love of motorcycles comes from his dad, who is a Mountain Bike Hall of Fame member.
- Tomac entered and won his first pro race in 2010. This made him the first rider in history to win his debut pro race.
- Since then, he has won championships in both 250MX and 450MX.
- Tomac began racing in the 250 class. In 2014, he moved up to 450MX. This class is the highest level of racing.

Eli Tomac races around the track at the Lucas Oil Pro Motocross Championship in 2019.

- In 2019, Tomac won the 450 class in the Lucas Oil Pro Motocross Championship for the third time in a row. He is only the fourth person to do this.

- Tomac also races in supercross events. In supercross, racers do 20 laps around a track inside a large stadium.

CHAPTER 4

SAFETY

Motocross racing is wild and fast. Riders wear safety gear to help prevent injuries. The most important piece of gear is the helmet. It fits snugly over the rider's head. A chin strap holds it in place.

LEARN MORE HERE!

A motocross helmet's long visor helps block the sun.

Goggles protect the rider's face and eyes. The lenses are **shatterproof**. Gloves, boots, and thick clothing cover the rest of the body. They protect the rider from flying dirt and rocks.

DID YOU KNOW?

Motocross racers wear steel-toed boots. These boots protect the feet. They also support the ankles on landings.

RACING GEAR

helmet
neck brace
goggles
chest protection
gloves
knee guards
boots

MAKING CONNECTIONS

TEXT-TO-SELF

Would you like to try riding through a motocross course? Why or why not?

TEXT-TO-TEXT

Have you read books about other kinds of racing? What kinds of tracks or vehicles do those races use?

TEXT-TO-WORLD

How might racing on a track inside a stadium be different from racing outdoors on rough ground?

GLOSSARY

closed-loop – forming a complete loop, so racers start and end at the same place.

cross-country – taking place across fields or rough ground instead of along a smooth track.

heat – one part or round of a race.

import – to bring something in from another country.

moto – a heat in a motocross race. Each race has two motos. Each moto lasts for 30 minutes, plus two more laps.

obstacle – something that blocks the way.

shatterproof – designed to resist breaking.

INDEX

ONLINE RESOURCES

popbooksonline.com

Scan this code* and others like it while you read, or visit the website below to make this book pop!

popbooksonline.com/motocross

*Scanning QR codes requires a web-enabled smart device with a QR code reader app and a camera.